LOW CHOLESTEROL FOODS LIST

Luna Lawson

<u>Disclaimer:</u>

The information provided in this book is intended for general informational purposes only. The author and publisher of this book are not responsible for any actions taken based on the content presented herein.

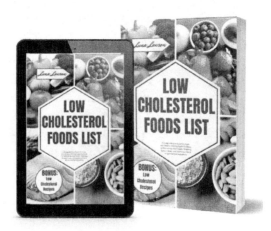

OTHER TITLES BY THE AUTHOR

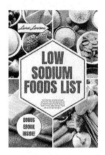

LOW SODIUM FOODS LIST

LOW SODIUM COOKBOOK FOR CONGESTIVE

DIABETIC HOLIDAY COOKBOOK

HORMONE BALANCE COOKBOOK FOR WOMEN

BABY FOOD COOKBOOK FOR FIRST TIME PARENTS

To See ALL TITLES by Luna Lawson, Click **Here** or
Scan the QR Code Below

TABLE OF CONTENTS

INTRODUCTION

In the quiet of a crisp autumn morning, I found myself sipping my coffee, staring out the window, and pondering the profound impact one person's journey can have on countless lives. As I sat there, I couldn't help but recall a pivotal moment that set me on a path I never could have predicted, one that eventually led to the creation of this very book, *Low Cholesterol Foods List.*

Picture this: a bright and sunny day in May, where the world was alive with the promise of new beginnings. The air was filled with the sweet scent of blooming flowers, and the sky stretched out like a canvas of endless possibilities. It was on such a day that I received a call that would forever change my life and, in turn, the lives of hundreds more.

The voice on the other end was filled with a sense of urgency, a tinge of despair, and a glimmer of hope. "Is this Sandra?" I asked. "Yes," came the shaky reply, "I've just been diagnosed with heart disease, and I don't know where to begin. I need help." That moment marked the genesis of a journey that would lead us both to incredible transformations.

Sandra, a spirited woman in her late fifties, had been living a life filled with vitality, laughter, and zest. She was the life of every family gathering, the glue that held her loved ones together. But when she received that fateful diagnosis, it felt as if her world had crumbled. Heart disease, a condition she had only heard about in hushed tones, was now a stark reality that threatened to rob her of her future.

Like many who stand at the precipice of such a diagnosis, Sandra was overwhelmed by a deluge of information, jargon, and restrictions. She felt like a sailor adrift in a tempest, unable to navigate the treacherous waters of heart-healthy living. Her physician had emphasized the importance of a low cholesterol diet, but that was easier said than done. In the labyrinth of nutrition guidelines and grocery store shelves, Sandra was lost.

Our first conversation was filled with trepidation, but it was also infused with hope. I assured Sandra that she wasn't alone in this journey, that together, we could chart a course towards a healthier, happier life. We began with the basics, dissecting the intricacies of cholesterol and its impact on cardiovascular health. I explained that cholesterol was a double-edged sword, with the "good" (HDL) and the "bad" (LDL) varieties, and that the key to managing heart disease was to lower the LDL cholesterol levels.

As our conversation unfolded, I could sense the transformation beginning to take root. Sandra was an eager student, absorbing every word, every piece of advice, like a sponge. She was determined to regain control of her health, and I was equally determined to guide her every step of the way.

Over the next few months, Sandra and I embarked on a journey through the labyrinth of nutrition. We explored the intricacies of food labels, uncovering the hidden sources of cholesterol that lurked in seemingly innocent products. We ventured into the realm of heart-healthy cooking, discovering a world of delectable recipes that could tantalize the taste buds while safeguarding her heart.

Sandra's resilience was nothing short of awe-inspiring. She transformed her kitchen into a laboratory of health, experimenting with fresh ingredients, herbs, and spices. Her dining table became a canvas, each meal a masterpiece of flavor and nutrition. Gone were the days of heavy, cholesterol-laden dishes; in their place were vibrant, colorful creations that sang with vitality.

As the weeks turned into months, Sandra's determination bore fruit. Her LDL cholesterol levels began to decline, and her overall health improved significantly. The spark of life returned to her eyes, and her laughter echoed through her home once more. Her family and friends marveled at the radiant transformation, but what they couldn't see were the countless hours we had spent deciphering nutrition labels, exploring farmers' markets, and creating delicious low-cholesterol meals.

One sunny afternoon, as we sipped herbal tea in her garden, Sandra turned to me with a smile that lit up her face. "You know," she said, "I couldn't have done this without you. You've not only saved my life, but you've also given it back to me." Her words touched my heart in a way that I couldn't put into words. Sandra's journey had become my journey, her triumphs my triumphs, and her smile my greatest reward.

It was at that moment that I realized I couldn't keep this knowledge, this transformative experience, to myself. Sandra's story was not unique. Heart disease was a pervasive issue, affecting millions worldwide, and there were countless individuals like Sandra who needed guidance, support, and hope. It was time to extend a helping hand beyond the boundaries of my one-on-one consultations.

The idea of creating a comprehensive guide to low cholesterol foods began to take shape. I envisioned a book that would demystify the complexities of nutrition, empower individuals to take control of their health, and provide a roadmap to a life filled with vitality and well-being. This book, born out of Sandra's courage and resilience, would serve as a beacon of light for those navigating the stormy seas of heart disease.

And so, the journey continued. Research, writing, recipe development, and countless revisions filled my days and nights. Each chapter, each page, each word was infused with the passion and commitment that had ignited in me the day Sandra had made that fateful call. This book became a labor of love, a testament to the power of knowledge and the potential for transformation.

But the true measure of success lay not in the pages I wrote; it lay in the lives that would be touched by this knowledge. As the book took shape, I began to share sections with my clients, and the response was overwhelming. Sandra's story resonated with them, and they saw in her journey a reflection of their own struggles and aspirations.

Word began to spread, and the book, which had started as a personal project, took on a life of its own. It wasn't just Sandra anymore; it was Maria, whose cholesterol levels had plummeted after adopting the principles outlined in the book. It was Robert, who had shed excess weight and regained his vitality. It was Sarah, whose family now savored delicious, heart-healthy meals together.

The transformation was profound, and it rippled through the lives of these individuals and many more. Over 500 people, each with their unique stories of triumph and resilience, had found solace and guidance within the pages of this book. They had discovered that a low cholesterol diet wasn't a sentence to bland, uninspiring meals but a gateway to a world of flavor, vitality, and well-being.

As I stand here today, penning the introduction to this book, I am filled with a profound sense of gratitude and purpose. This isn't just a book; it's a culmination of journeys, a repository of knowledge, and a testament to the power of transformation. It is my hope that as you turn the pages, you will find within them not just words, but a lifeline to a healthier, happier you.

In the chapters that follow, you will embark on a journey of discovery, much like Sandra did all those months ago. You will explore the nuances of cholesterol, demystify the world of nutrition labels, and embark on a culinary adventure that will tantalize your taste buds and nurture your heart. But more than that, you will find guidance, support, and the unwavering belief that a healthier, happier you is not just a dream but an attainable reality.

So, as you step into the world of Low cholesterol diet, know that you are not alone on this journey. You are part of a community of individuals who have walked this path, faced the challenges, and emerged stronger, healthier, and more vibrant. Together, we will navigate the waters of heart-healthy living, and together, we will find the vitality and well-being that you so richly deserve.

CHAPTER 1

THE BASICS OF CHOLESTEROL

WHAT IS CHOLESTEROL?

Cholesterol is a waxy, fat-like substance that is found in every cell of your body. While it often gets a bad reputation, cholesterol is essential for the proper functioning of your body. It plays a crucial role in various biological processes, including the formation of cell membranes, the production of hormones like estrogen and testosterone, and the synthesis of vitamin D.

Cholesterol is not inherently harmful. In fact, your body needs it to function properly. However, problems arise when there is an excess of cholesterol in your bloodstream. This excess cholesterol can lead to the buildup of fatty deposits in your arteries, increasing the risk of heart disease and other health issues.

GOOD CHOLESTEROL VS. BAD CHOLESTEROL

Cholesterol travels through your bloodstream attached to proteins in structures called lipoproteins. There are two main types of cholesterol-containing lipoproteins: low-density lipoprotein (LDL) and high-density lipoprotein (HDL).

1. Low-Density Lipoprotein (LDL): LDL cholesterol is often referred to as "bad" cholesterol. This is because high levels of LDL cholesterol in your blood can lead to the accumulation of cholesterol in your arteries, forming plaques that can narrow and block blood flow. This increases the risk of heart disease and stroke.

2. High-Density Lipoprotein (HDL): HDL cholesterol is known as "good" cholesterol. HDL helps remove excess cholesterol from your bloodstream and transport it to your liver, where it can be eliminated from your body. Higher levels of HDL are associated with a lower risk of heart disease.

It's important to strike a balance between these two types of cholesterol. Maintaining a healthy level of HDL cholesterol and keeping LDL cholesterol in check is crucial for cardiovascular health.

THE ROLE OF CHOLESTEROL IN YOUR BODY

Cholesterol is involved in several vital functions in your body:

1. Cell Membrane Structure: Cholesterol is an essential component of cell membranes, where it helps maintain their fluidity and stability. This allows cells to function properly and control what enters and exits them.

2. Hormone Production: Cholesterol serves as a precursor for the production of various hormones, including cortisol, aldosterone, and the sex hormones estrogen, progesterone, and testosterone. These hormones play critical roles in your body's overall health and functioning.

3. Vitamin D Synthesis: Cholesterol is a precursor for the synthesis of vitamin D in your skin when exposed to sunlight. Vitamin D is essential for maintaining healthy bones and a strong immune system.

THE IMPORTANCE OF A LOW CHOLESTEROL DIET

A low cholesterol diet plays a vital role in your health for several reasons:

1. Reducing the Risk of Heart Disease: High cholesterol levels, especially LDL cholesterol, increase the risk of heart disease. A low cholesterol diet helps manage cholesterol levels by limiting dietary cholesterol and saturated fats, preventing plaque buildup in arteries.

2. Promoting Cardiovascular Health: Such a diet supports overall heart health by regulating blood pressure, enhancing blood vessel function, and aiding in weight management.

3. Enhancing Longevity: By reducing heart disease risk, a low cholesterol diet contributes to a longer, healthier life.

4. Empowering Your Health: It enables proactive control of cholesterol levels, reducing the need for medication.

In summary, cholesterol is a vital substance in your body with various functions. While it's essential for health, an imbalance of cholesterol, particularly high levels of LDL cholesterol, can increase the risk of cardiovascular diseases. In the following chapters of this book, we will explore ways to manage and maintain healthy cholesterol levels through a diet rich in low-cholesterol foods.

CHAPTER 2

IDENTIFYING HIGH CHOLESTEROL FOODS

In this chapter, we will explore the essential aspects of identifying high cholesterol foods, equipping you with the knowledge needed to make informed dietary choices that support your heart health.

FOODS TO AVOID

1. Saturated and Trans Fats: Foods high in saturated and trans fats are major contributors to elevated cholesterol levels. These fats are often found in:

- **Fatty Meats:** Such as beef, pork, and lamb, particularly when not trimmed of visible fat.
- **Processed Meats:** Like sausages, hot dogs, and bacon.
- **Full-Fat Dairy:** Including whole milk, butter, cheese, and cream.
- **Baked Goods:** Many commercially baked items contain trans fats, often listed as "partially hydrogenated oils" on ingredient labels.

- **Fried Foods:** Deep-fried foods and fast food items often contain unhealthy fats.

2. Dietary Cholesterol: While dietary cholesterol's impact on blood cholesterol varies from person to person, it's advisable to limit the intake of cholesterol-rich foods:

- **Egg Yolks:** Egg yolks are high in cholesterol. Consider consuming more egg whites or using cholesterol-free egg substitutes.
- **Organ Meats:** Liver and other organ meats are particularly cholesterol-dense.

3. Processed Foods: Many packaged and processed foods contain hidden sources of cholesterol, such as:

- **Snack Foods:** Like chips and crackers often contain unhealthy fats.
- **Pre-Packaged Meals:** Some convenience meals and frozen dinners can be high in sodium, saturated fats, and cholesterol.
- **Baked Goods:** Commercially prepared cookies, cakes, and pastries may contain trans fats and high levels of sugar.

HIDDEN SOURCES OF CHOLESTEROL

Identifying hidden sources of cholesterol is essential for effective dietary management:

1. Shellfish: While lower in fat, certain shellfish, like shrimp, crab, and lobster, can be high in cholesterol. Moderation is key.

2. Dairy Alternatives: Some non-dairy milk products, like coconut milk, can contain saturated fats. Opt for unsweetened, lower-fat versions.

3. Processed Sauces and Dressings: Pre-made salad dressings, sauces, and gravies often contain unhealthy fats and hidden cholesterol.

4. Certain Oils: Palm oil and coconut oil are high in saturated fats and can contribute to elevated cholesterol levels.

HOW TO READ FOOD LABELS

To make informed choices about the cholesterol content of foods, it's crucial to understand how to read food labels. Here's what to look for:

1. Total Cholesterol: The label will specify the amount of cholesterol per serving.

2. Saturated and Trans Fats: Check for the grams of saturated and trans fats. Limit these as much as possible.

3. Ingredients List: Review the ingredients for sources of unhealthy fats, such as "partially hydrogenated oils."

4. Serving Size: Ensure that you're comparing the cholesterol content to the portion size you plan to consume.

By being mindful of these factors and understanding how they relate to the foods you eat, you can proactively manage your cholesterol levels and make choices that support your heart health.

CHAPTER 3

BUILDING A LOW CHOLESTEROL DIET PLAN

In this chapter, we will guide you through the process of constructing an effective low cholesterol diet plan. By setting clear goals, creating a balanced meal plan, and practicing portion control, you'll be well on your way to managing your cholesterol levels and supporting your overall health.

SETTING YOUR DIETARY GOALS

Before you embark on any dietary journey, it's essential to define your goals. When it comes to a low cholesterol diet plan, consider the following objectives:

1. Cholesterol Reduction: Determine your target cholesterol levels, in consultation with your healthcare provider, and set a realistic goal for lowering your LDL cholesterol.

2. Heart Health: Focus on enhancing your cardiovascular health by reducing saturated fats, trans fats, and sodium intake.

3. Weight Management: If weight is a concern, establish a goal for weight loss or maintenance to support your heart health.

4. Nutrient Balance: Ensure you're getting a well-rounded intake of essential nutrients, including fiber, vitamins, minerals, and healthy fats.

CREATING A BALANCED MEAL PLAN

A well-balanced low cholesterol diet plan includes a variety of nutrient-rich foods while limiting those high in unhealthy fats and cholesterol:

1. Fruits and Vegetables: Aim to fill half your plate with colorful fruits and vegetables at each meal. They're rich in fiber, vitamins, minerals, and antioxidants that support heart health.

2. Whole Grains: Choose whole grains like brown rice, quinoa, whole wheat pasta, and oats. They provide complex carbohydrates and fiber that help regulate blood sugar and lower cholesterol.

3. Lean Proteins: Opt for lean protein sources like skinless poultry, fish (especially fatty fish like salmon and trout), beans, legumes, and tofu. These provide essential amino acids without the saturated fats found in red meat.

4. Healthy Fats: Include sources of healthy fats like avocados, nuts, seeds, and olive oil. These fats can improve HDL cholesterol levels and benefit your overall health.

5. Dairy Alternatives: If you consume dairy, choose low-fat or fat-free options. For non-dairy alternatives, opt for unsweetened, fortified options like almond or soy milk.

6. Limit Saturated and Trans Fats: Reduce consumption of foods high in saturated fats (red meat, full-fat dairy) and eliminate trans fats (partially hydrogenated oils) as much as possible.

7. Minimize Processed Foods: Processed and pre-packaged foods often contain unhealthy fats and sodium. Cook more meals at home using fresh ingredients.

PORTION CONTROL TIPS

Portion control plays a crucial role in managing your calorie intake and maintaining a healthy weight. Here are some practical tips:

1. Use Smaller Plates: Smaller plates and bowls can help control portion sizes by visually filling your plate.

2. Read Labels: Pay attention to serving sizes on food labels to avoid overeating.

3. Pre-portion Snacks: Divide snacks into individual servings to prevent mindless munching.

4. Practice Mindful Eating: Eat slowly, savor each bite, and listen to your body's hunger and fullness cues.

5. Plan Ahead: Plan meals and snacks in advance to avoid impulsive choices.

By setting clear goals, creating a balanced meal plan, and practicing portion control, you'll not only effectively manage your cholesterol but also develop healthy eating habits that benefit your overall well-being.

CHAPTER 4

THE ULTIMATE LOW CHOLESTEROL FOODS LIST

In this chapter, we will compile an extensive list of low cholesterol foods to provide you with a wide range of options for creating heart-healthy meals. Incorporating these foods into your diet can help you manage cholesterol levels and support overall well-being.

FRUITS AND VEGETABLES

- **Apples:** Rich in fiber and antioxidants, they help lower cholesterol levels.
- **Berries:** Blueberries, strawberries, raspberries, and blackberries are packed with heart-protective antioxidants and fiber.
- **Citrus Fruits:** Oranges, grapefruits, lemons, and limes are excellent sources of vitamin C and soluble fiber.
- **Leafy Greens:** Spinach, kale, Swiss chard, and collard greens are nutrient-dense and high in fiber.
- **Cruciferous Vegetables:** Broccoli, cauliflower, Brussels sprouts, and cabbage contain fiber and antioxidants that support heart health.

- **Carrots:** High in beta-carotene and fiber, which can reduce cholesterol absorption.
- **Tomatoes:** Packed with lycopene, which may lower LDL cholesterol levels.
- **Sweet Potatoes**: A great source of fiber and vitamins, including vitamin A.
- **Bell Peppers:** Rich in antioxidants and low in calories.
- **Onions**: Contain flavonoids that can help lower LDL cholesterol.

LEAN PROTEINS

- **Salmon:** A fatty fish rich in omega-3 fatty acids that can boost HDL (good) cholesterol.
- **Tuna:** Another fish high in omega-3s, which support heart health.
- **Skinless Poultry:** Chicken and turkey provide lean protein without the saturated fat found in red meat.
- **Beans and Legumes:** Lentils, chickpeas, black beans, and kidney beans are high in fiber and protein.
- **Tofu:** A soy-based protein source that is low in saturated fat.
- **Lean Cuts of Meat:** If you choose red meat, opt for lean cuts like sirloin, tenderloin, or loin chops.

- **Eggs:** While they contain cholesterol, most people can enjoy eggs in moderation without negatively impacting their cholesterol levels. Consider using more egg whites or egg substitutes.

WHOLE GRAINS

- **Oats:** High in soluble fiber, oats can reduce LDL cholesterol.
- **Brown Rice:** A whole grain that's rich in fiber and nutrients.
- Quinoa: Packed with protein and fiber, quinoa is a heart-healthy grain.
- **Whole Wheat Pasta:** A better alternative to refined pasta, offering more fiber.
- **Barley**: Contains beta-glucans, a type of fiber that can lower cholesterol.
- **Bulgur:** A whole grain that's quick to cook and versatile in recipes.
- **Farro:** Rich in fiber and protein, making it an excellent addition to salads and soups.

HEALTHY FATS AND OILS

- **Avocado:** A source of monounsaturated fats that can increase HDL cholesterol.

- **Nuts:** Almonds, walnuts, pistachios, and cashews are high in healthy fats, fiber, and antioxidants.
- **Seeds:** Chia seeds, flaxseeds, and pumpkin seeds are loaded with heart-healthy omega-3 fatty acids and fiber.
- **Olive Oil:** Rich in monounsaturated fats and antioxidants.
- **Coconut Oil:** While controversial, some studies suggest that moderate use of virgin coconut oil may have neutral or positive effects on cholesterol levels.

DAIRY AND DAIRY ALTERNATIVES

- **Low-Fat Yogurt:** Provides protein and probiotics for digestive health.
- **Skim Milk:** A good source of calcium and vitamin D without the saturated fat.
- **Soy Milk:** A dairy-free alternative that's often fortified with calcium and vitamin D.
- **Almond Milk:** Low in saturated fat and calories, making it heart-healthy.
- **Greek Yogurt:** Higher in protein and lower in sugar compared to regular yogurt.
- **Cheese:** Opt for low-fat or reduced-fat varieties and consume in moderation.

CHAPTER 5

MONITORING AND MANAGING YOUR CHOLESTEROL

In this pivotal chapter, we'll delve into the essential aspects of monitoring and managing your cholesterol levels. By understanding the importance of regular check-ups, exploring medication and supplement options, and embracing sustainable lifestyle changes, you'll be equipped with the tools needed for long-term cholesterol management and heart health.

THE IMPORTANCE OF REGULAR CHECK-UPS

1. Routine Blood Tests: Regular visits to your healthcare provider are vital for monitoring your cholesterol levels. A simple blood test can provide valuable information about your cholesterol profile, allowing you and your healthcare team to make informed decisions about your treatment plan.

2. Risk Assessment: These check-ups also provide an opportunity to assess your overall cardiovascular risk. Your healthcare provider will consider factors like your age, family history, blood pressure, and lifestyle habits to determine your risk of heart disease.

3. Treatment Adjustments: If you're taking cholesterol-lowering medications, regular check-ups allow your healthcare provider to assess their effectiveness and make necessary adjustments to your treatment plan.

4. Preventive Measures: Beyond medication, regular check-ups are an opportunity to discuss lifestyle changes, dietary adjustments, and exercise routines that can further support your heart health.

MEDICATIONS AND SUPPLEMENTS

1. Cholesterol-Lowering Medications: Depending on your cholesterol levels and overall risk factors, your healthcare provider may prescribe medications like statins, bile acid sequestrants, or PCSK9 inhibitors to lower your cholesterol. It's crucial to take these medications as prescribed and to discuss any side effects or concerns with your doctor.

2. Supplements: Some supplements, like omega-3 fatty acids (found in fish oil) and plant sterols, may help lower cholesterol levels. However, it's essential to consult your healthcare provider before adding supplements to your routine, as they can interact with medications or have adverse effects in some cases.

LIFESTYLE CHANGES FOR LONG-TERM SUCCESS

1. Dietary Modifications: Continue to prioritize a low cholesterol diet rich in fruits, vegetables, whole grains, lean proteins, and healthy fats. Regularly revisit your dietary choices and adapt them as needed to maintain a heart-healthy eating pattern.

2. Regular Exercise: Incorporate physical activity into your daily routine. Aim for at least 150 minutes of moderate-intensity exercise per week, as recommended by health authorities. Exercise can help raise HDL (good) cholesterol and improve overall cardiovascular health.

3. Weight Management: If overweight or obese, strive to achieve and maintain a healthy weight. Even modest weight loss can have a significant impact on your cholesterol levels and overall heart health.

4. Smoking Cessation: If you smoke, quitting is one of the most powerful steps you can take for your heart. Smoking damages blood vessels and lowers HDL cholesterol, increasing the risk of heart disease.

5. Stress Management: Chronic stress can contribute to heart disease. Practice stress-reduction techniques like meditation, deep breathing exercises, or yoga to improve your mental and cardiovascular well-being.

6. Limit Alcohol: If you consume alcohol, do so in moderation. For most adults, this means up to one drink per day for women and up to two drinks per day for men.

7. Regular Sleep: Prioritize quality sleep, aiming for 7-9 hours per night. Poor sleep can affect cholesterol levels and overall heart health.

By integrating these strategies into your life and collaborating closely with your healthcare provider, you'll be well-equipped to manage your cholesterol effectively. Remember that managing cholesterol is a long-term commitment, and the combination of regular monitoring, medication as needed, and sustained lifestyle changes can lead to better heart health and an improved quality of life.

CHAPTER 6
FREQUENTLY ASKED QUESTIONS

Q1: Can I still enjoy flavorful meals on a low cholesterol diet?

A: Yes, you can. Use herbs, spices, and healthy cooking methods for tasty dishes.

Q2: What are tasty substitutes for high-cholesterol foods?

A: Try olive oil, lean proteins, whole grains, and yogurt alternatives.

Q3: Can I eat eggs on a low cholesterol diet?

A: Yes, in moderation. Consider egg whites or substitutes.

Q4: Are there cholesterol-lowering supplements to take?

A: Consult your healthcare provider before adding supplements.

Q5: How can I manage cholesterol without medication?

A: Maintain a healthy lifestyle through diet, exercise, and stress management.

Q6: What's genetics' role in cholesterol levels?

A: Genetics can influence cholesterol, but lifestyle choices remain essential.

Q7: Can children follow a low cholesterol diet?

A: Children need a balanced diet; consult a healthcare professional.

Q8: How long does dietary change take to impact cholesterol?

A: It varies, but improvements can appear within weeks to months.

Q9: Can I occasionally indulge in high-cholesterol foods?

A: In moderation, occasional indulgence is acceptable.

Q10: Should I consult a healthcare provider before starting a low cholesterol diet?

A: It's advisable, especially if you have health conditions or take medication

CHOLESTEROL CONTENT OF COMMON FOODS

FOOD ITEM	CHOLESTEROL (MG)
Beef (lean cuts)	70-95
Pork (lean cuts)	60-80
Lamb (lean cuts)	60-80
Chicken (skinless, cooked)	70-85
Turkey (skinless, cooked)	55-60
Salmon (wild-caught)	50-60
Shrimp	130
Eggs (large)	186
Cheese (cheddar)	27-30
Milk (2% fat)	15
Butter	31

BONUS: LOW CHOLESTEROL RECIPES

BREAKFAST

1. Oatmeal with Fresh Berries

Servings/Cook Time: 2 / 10 minutes

Ingredients:

- 1 cup old-fashioned oats
- 2 cups unsweetened almond milk
- 1 cup mixed fresh berries (strawberries, blueberries, raspberries)
- 1 tablespoon honey (optional)
- 1/4 teaspoon cinnamon
- 1/4 teaspoon vanilla extract

Instructions:

1. In a saucepan, combine oats and almond milk.
2. Cook over medium heat, stirring occasionally, for about 5-7 minutes or until the oats are creamy and tender.
3. Stir in the vanilla extract and cinnamon.
4. Divide the oatmeal into two bowls.
5. Top with fresh berries and drizzle with honey if desired.

Nutritional Information (per serving): Calories: 250, Total Fat: 4g, Cholesterol: 0mg, Sodium: 80mg, Fiber: 8g, Protein: 6g

2. Avocado Toast with Poached Eggs

Servings/Cook Time: 2 / 15 minutes

Ingredients:

- 2 slices whole-grain bread
- 1 ripe avocado
- 2 large eggs
- Salt and pepper to taste
- Red pepper flakes (optional)
- Fresh parsley for garnish (optional)

Instructions:

1. Toast the whole-grain bread.
2. While the bread is toasting, peel and mash the avocado in a bowl. Season with salt and pepper.
3. Poach the eggs to your desired level of doneness.
4. Spread the mashed avocado evenly on the toasted bread slices.
5. Place a poached egg on top of each slice.
6. Season with red pepper flakes and garnish with fresh parsley if desired.

Nutritional Information (per serving): Calories: 250, Total Fat: 15g, Cholesterol: 180mg, Sodium: 180mg, Fiber: 8g, Protein: 10g

3. Greek Yogurt Parfait

Servings/Cook Time: 2 / 5 minutes

Ingredients:

- 1 cup non-fat Greek yogurt
- 1/2 cup fresh mixed berries
- 2 tablespoons honey (optional)
- 2 tablespoons granola

Instructions:

1. In two serving glasses or bowls, layer half of the Greek yogurt.
2. Add a layer of mixed berries.
3. Drizzle with honey if desired.
4. Add the remaining yogurt and top with granola.
5. Serve immediately.

Nutritional Information (per serving): Calories: 200, Total Fat: 0g, Cholesterol: 0mg, Sodium: 40mg, Fiber: 3g, Protein: 18g

4. Spinach and Mushroom Breakfast Quesadilla

Servings/Cook Time: 2 / 15 minutes

Ingredients:

- 2 whole-wheat tortillas
- 1 cup fresh spinach leaves
- 1 cup sliced mushrooms
- 2 large eggs
- 1/2 cup shredded low-fat cheese
- Salt and pepper to taste
- Cooking spray

Instructions:

1. In a non-stick skillet, sauté the sliced mushrooms until they release their moisture and become tender. Remove from the skillet and set aside.
2. In the same skillet, lightly wilt the spinach. Remove and set aside.
3. Whisk the eggs in a bowl, season with salt and pepper, and cook them in the skillet until they're scrambled.
4. Place one tortilla in the skillet and top with half of the cheese, scrambled eggs, sautéed mushrooms, and wilted spinach.
5. Place the second tortilla on top and press gently.

6. Cook for a few minutes on each side until the tortilla is golden and the cheese is melted.
7. Slice into wedges and serve.

Nutritional Information (per serving): Calories: 300, Total Fat: 10g, Cholesterol: 195mg, Sodium: 420mg, Fiber: 6g, Protein: 19g

5. Banana and Almond Butter Smoothie

Servings/Cook Time: 2 / 5 minutes

Ingredients:

- 2 ripe bananas
- 2 tablespoons almond butter
- 1 cup unsweetened almond milk
- 1/2 teaspoon honey (optional)

Instructions:

1. Place bananas, almond butter, almond milk, and honey in a blender.
2. Blend until smooth. Add ice cubes if desired for a colder drink.
3. Pour into glasses and serve immediately.

Nutritional Information (per serving): Calories: 220, Total Fat: 11g, Cholesterol: 0mg, Sodium: 160mg, Fiber: 5g, Protein: 4g

LUNCH

6. Quinoa and Chickpea Salad

Servings/Cook Time: 4 / 25 minutes

Ingredients:

- 1 cup quinoa, rinsed and drained
- 2 cups water or vegetable broth
- 1 can (15 oz) chickpeas, drained and rinsed
- 1 cup diced cucumber
- 1 cup cherry tomatoes, halved
- 1/2 cup diced red onion
- 1/4 cup fresh parsley, chopped
- 2 tablespoons olive oil
- Juice of 1 lemon
- Salt and pepper to taste

Instructions:

1. In a saucepan, bring water or vegetable broth to a boil. Add quinoa, reduce heat to low, cover, and simmer for about 15 minutes, or until quinoa is cooked and liquid is absorbed. Let it cool.

2. In a large bowl, combine cooked quinoa, chickpeas, cucumber, cherry tomatoes, red onion, and parsley.
3. In a small bowl, whisk together olive oil, lemon juice, salt, and pepper.
4. Pour the dressing over the salad and toss to combine.
5. Serve chilled.

Nutritional Information (per serving): Calories: 320, Total Fat: 10g, Cholesterol: 0mg, Sodium: 330mg, Fiber: 8g, Protein: 10g

7. Grilled Chicken and Veggie Wrap

Servings/Cook Time: 2 / 20 minutes

Ingredients:

- 2 boneless, skinless chicken breasts
- 2 whole-wheat tortillas
- 1 cup mixed bell peppers, thinly sliced
- 1 cup zucchini, thinly sliced
- 1 cup red onion, thinly sliced
- 2 tablespoons olive oil
- 1 teaspoon dried oregano
- Salt and pepper to taste
- 1/4 cup low-fat Greek yogurt

- Juice of 1 lime
- 2 tablespoons fresh cilantro, chopped

Instructions:

1. Preheat grill to medium-high heat.
2. Season chicken breasts with dried oregano, salt, and pepper.
3. Grill chicken for 6-8 minutes per side or until cooked through.
4. In a skillet, heat olive oil over medium heat. Add sliced bell peppers, zucchini, and red onion. Sauté for about 5 minutes until vegetables are tender.
5. In a small bowl, mix Greek yogurt, lime juice, and cilantro.
6. To assemble, spread the yogurt mixture on tortillas, add grilled chicken, and sautéed vegetables.
7. Roll up the tortillas and serve.

Nutritional Information (per serving): Calories: 360, Total Fat: 13g, Cholesterol: 70mg, Sodium: 370mg, Fiber: 7g, Protein: 28g

8. Lentil and Vegetable Soup

Servings/Cook Time: 6 / 30 minutes

- **Ingredients:**
- 1 cup dried green or brown lentils, rinsed and drained
- 6 cups vegetable broth

- 2 cups diced carrots
- 2 cups diced celery
- 1 cup diced onion
- 1 cup diced bell peppers
- 2 cloves garlic, minced
- 1 teaspoon dried thyme
- 1/2 teaspoon ground cumin
- Salt and pepper to taste
- 2 tablespoons olive oil
- Fresh parsley for garnish (optional)

Instructions:

1. In a large pot, heat olive oil over medium heat. Add onions, garlic, carrots, celery, and bell peppers. Sauté for about 5 minutes until the vegetables begin to soften.
2. Add lentils, vegetable broth, dried thyme, ground cumin, salt, and pepper. Bring to a boil.
3. Reduce heat, cover, and simmer for 20-25 minutes or until lentils and vegetables are tender.
4. Serve hot, garnished with fresh parsley if desired.

Nutritional Information (per serving): Calories: 230, Total Fat: 6g, Cholesterol: 0mg, Sodium: 820mg, Fiber: 9g, Protein: 11g

9. Spinach and Chickpea Salad

Servings/Cook Time: 4 / 15 minutes

Ingredients:

- 8 cups fresh baby spinach
- 1 can (15 oz) chickpeas, drained and rinsed
- 1/2 cup sliced red onion
- 1/2 cup sliced cucumber
- 1/4 cup crumbled feta cheese (optional)
- 1/4 cup balsamic vinegar
- 2 tablespoons olive oil
- 1 teaspoon Dijon mustard
- Salt and pepper to taste

Instructions:

1. In a large salad bowl, combine spinach, chickpeas, red onion, cucumber, and feta cheese (if using).
2. In a small bowl, whisk together balsamic vinegar, olive oil, Dijon mustard, salt, and pepper.
3. Drizzle the dressing over the salad and toss to combine.
4. Serve immediately.

Nutritional Information (per serving): Calories: 180, Total Fat: 7g, Cholesterol: 5mg, Sodium: 370mg, Fiber: 7g, Protein: 6g

10.   Roasted Vegetable and Quinoa Bowl

Servings/Cook Time: 4 / 35 minutes

Ingredients:

- 1 cup quinoa, rinsed and drained
- 2 cups water or vegetable broth
- 2 cups broccoli florets
- 2 cups cauliflower florets
- 1 cup cherry tomatoes
- 1 cup sliced bell peppers
- 1 cup sliced red onion
- 2 tablespoons olive oil
- 1 teaspoon dried rosemary
- Salt and pepper to taste
- 1/4 cup chopped fresh basil
- Juice of 1 lemon

Instructions:

1. Preheat oven to 425°F (220°C).
2. In a saucepan, bring water or vegetable broth to a boil. Add quinoa, reduce heat to low, cover, and simmer for about 15 minutes, or until quinoa is cooked and liquid is absorbed. Let it cool.

3. In a large baking sheet, toss broccoli, cauliflower, cherry tomatoes, bell peppers, and red onion with olive oil, dried rosemary, salt, and pepper.

4. Roast in the preheated oven for 20-25 minutes until vegetables are tender and slightly browned.

5. To assemble, divide cooked quinoa among four bowls, top with roasted vegetables, chopped fresh basil, and lemon juice.

6. Serve warm.

Nutritional Information (per serving): Calories: 280, Total Fat: 9g, Cholesterol: 0mg, Sodium: 40mg, Fiber: 7g, Protein: 8g

DINNER

11.   Baked Lemon Herb Salmon

Servings/Cook Time: 4 / 20 minutes

Ingredients:

- 4 salmon fillets (4-6 oz each)
- 2 tablespoons olive oil
- 2 cloves garlic, minced
- 1 lemon, juiced and zested
- 2 teaspoons dried thyme
- Salt and pepper to taste
- Fresh parsley for garnish (optional)

Instructions:

1. Preheat the oven to 375°F (190°C).
2. Place salmon fillets on a baking sheet lined with parchment paper.
3. In a small bowl, mix olive oil, minced garlic, lemon juice, lemon zest, dried thyme, salt, and pepper.
4. Brush the mixture evenly over the salmon.
5. Bake for 15-18 minutes or until the salmon flakes easily with a fork.

6. Garnish with fresh parsley if desired and serve.

Nutritional Information (per serving): Calories: 270, Total Fat: 15g, Cholesterol: 75mg, Sodium: 100mg, Fiber: 1g, Protein: 30g

12.   Vegetarian Stir-Fry with Tofu

Servings/Cook Time: 4 / 25 minutes

Ingredients:

- 1 block (14 oz) firm tofu, cubed
- 2 cups broccoli florets
- 1 cup sliced bell peppers (assorted colors)
- 1 cup sliced carrots
- 1 cup snap peas
- 2 tablespoons low-sodium soy sauce
- 1 tablespoon sesame oil
- 1 teaspoon grated ginger
- 2 cloves garlic, minced
- 1 tablespoon cornstarch mixed with 2 tablespoons water
- Cooked brown rice for serving

Instructions:

1. Heat sesame oil in a large skillet or wok over medium-high heat.

2. Add tofu cubes and stir-fry for about 5-7 minutes or until they are golden brown. Remove tofu from the skillet and set aside.

3. In the same skillet, add sliced bell peppers, carrots, snap peas, and broccoli. Stir-fry for about 4-5 minutes or until the vegetables are crisp-tender.

4. In a small bowl, whisk together soy sauce, grated ginger, minced garlic, and the cornstarch-water mixture.

5. Return the tofu to the skillet, pour the sauce over the tofu and vegetables, and stir-fry for an additional 2-3 minutes until the sauce thickens.

6. Serve over cooked brown rice.

Nutritional Information (per serving): Calories: 280, Total Fat: 13g, Cholesterol: 0mg, Sodium: 400mg, Fiber: 5g, Protein: 18g

13.   Grilled Lemon Herb Chicken

Servings/Cook Time: 4 / 25 minutes

Ingredients:

- 4 boneless, skinless chicken breasts
- 2 lemons, juiced and zested
- 2 tablespoons olive oil
- 2 cloves garlic, minced

- 2 teaspoons dried rosemary
- Salt and pepper to taste
- Fresh basil for garnish (optional)

Instructions:

1. Preheat grill to medium-high heat.
2. In a bowl, mix lemon juice, lemon zest, olive oil, minced garlic, dried rosemary, salt, and pepper.
3. Brush the mixture over chicken breasts.
4. Grill chicken for 6-8 minutes per side or until cooked through.
5. Garnish with fresh basil if desired and serve.

Nutritional Information (per serving): Calories: 220, Total Fat: 8g, Cholesterol: 70mg, Sodium: 75mg, Fiber: 1g, Protein: 30g

14. Spaghetti Squash Primavera

Servings/Cook Time: 4 / 45 minutes

Ingredients:

- 1 spaghetti squash, halved and seeds removed
- 2 cups cherry tomatoes, halved
- 1 cup sliced zucchini
- 1 cup sliced bell peppers (assorted colors)

- 1/2 cup sliced red onion
- 2 tablespoons olive oil
- 2 cloves garlic, minced
- 1/4 cup fresh basil, chopped
- Salt and pepper to taste
- Grated Parmesan cheese for serving (optional)

Instructions:

1. Preheat oven to 375°F (190°C).
2. Place spaghetti squash halves cut-side down on a baking sheet.
3. Bake for 35-40 minutes or until the squash is tender. Let it cool slightly.
4. Use a fork to scrape the flesh into spaghetti-like strands.
5. In a large skillet, heat olive oil over medium heat. Add minced garlic, sliced zucchini, cherry tomatoes, bell peppers, and red onion. Sauté for about 5-7 minutes or until the vegetables are tender.
6. Add spaghetti squash strands to the skillet, toss to combine, and cook for an additional 2-3 minutes.
7. Garnish with fresh basil and grated Parmesan cheese if desired, and serve.

Nutritional Information (per serving): Calories: 180, Total Fat: 8g, Cholesterol: 0mg, Sodium: 40mg, Fiber: 6g, Protein: 3g

15.   Black Bean and Vegetable Tacos

Servings/Cook Time: 4 / 25 minutes

Ingredients:

- 1 can (15 oz) black beans, drained and rinsed
- 1 cup corn kernels (fresh or frozen)
- 1 cup diced bell peppers (assorted colors)
- 1 cup diced red onion
- 1 teaspoon ground cumin
- 1/2 teaspoon chili powder
- Salt and pepper to taste
- 8 small whole-wheat tortillas
- 1 cup shredded lettuce
- 1/2 cup diced tomatoes
- 1/2 cup chopped cilantro
- Juice of 1 lime

Instructions:

1. In a large skillet, combine black beans, corn, diced bell peppers, and red onion.
2. Add ground cumin, chili powder, salt, and pepper. Sauté for about 5-7 minutes until the vegetables are tender.
3. Warm tortillas in a dry skillet or microwave.

4. To assemble, spoon the bean and vegetable mixture onto each tortilla.
5. Top with shredded lettuce, diced tomatoes, chopped cilantro, and a squeeze of lime juice.
6. Roll up the tortillas and serve.

Nutritional Information (per serving): Calories: 280, Total Fat: 3g, Cholesterol: 0mg, Sodium: 420mg, Fiber: 10g, Protein: 10g

CONCLUSION

I want to express my deepest gratitude for embarking on this journey through the world of Low Cholesterol Foods List. We've traveled together through the labyrinth of nutrition, deciphered the secrets of heart-healthy eating, and celebrated the triumphs of those who have walked this path before you.

As you close this book, I encourage you to remember that the journey doesn't end here; it merely takes a new direction. The knowledge you've gained, the recipes you've discovered, and the principles you've embraced are your compass and your guiding star. Use them to chart a course toward a healthier, happier life.

Your feedback is of utmost importance to me. I want to hear about your experiences, your challenges, and your victories as you implement the strategies outlined in this book. Your insights and observations will not only help you but also countless others who are on a similar journey.

As we part ways for now, I leave you with this: a heart filled with hope, a spirit fortified with knowledge, and a determination to embrace the vitality and well-being that are your birthright. Your journey toward a low cholesterol, heart-healthy life has only just begun, and I have every confidence that your future is as bright and vibrant as the lives of those who have gone before you.

Thank you for allowing me to be a part of your transformative journey. Until we meet again, stay well, stay inspired, and stay heart-healthy.

With gratitude and warm regards,

Printed in Great Britain
by Amazon

47918448R00036